P9-BJU-187

this book is from the library of:

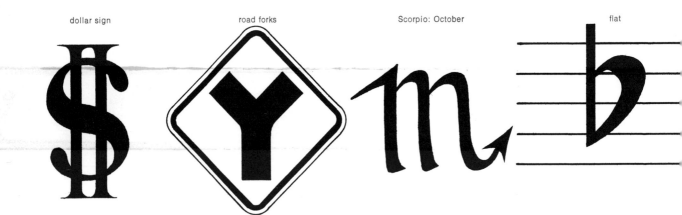

dollar sign   road forks   Scorpio: October   flat

rotary

ground to air: fuel required

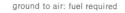
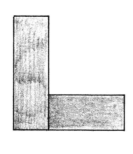

mathematical integral

a silent language

Walker and Company
720 Fifth Avenue
New York

written
designed and
illustrated by
JAN ADKINS

Copyright © 1978 by Jan Adkins, still at it.

First published in the United States of America in 1978 by the Walker Publishing Company, Inc. and simultaneously in Canada by Beaverbooks, Limited, Pickering, Ontario.

Trade ISBN: 0-8027-6330-8
Reinf. ISBN: 0-8027-6331-6

Library of Congress Catalog Card Number: 78-2977

Printed in the United States of America

10 9 8 7 6 5 4 3 2 1

for Grubster
Webster Roberts Peirce

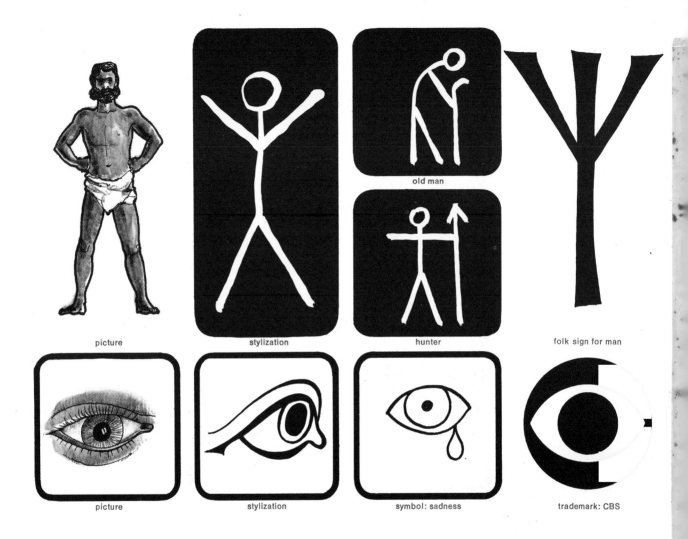

picture stylization old man hunter folk sign for man

picture stylization symbol: sadness trademark: CBS

The language of symbols has no words but it can shout warnings, give instructions, direct traffic, and play cards. Without words it can speak in a hundred languages ... all at once. Almost everyone understands it but no one speaks it. It is a silent, serious game played with pictures and it is all around you. You play it every day and you probably know more symbols than you think you do.

Some symbols are pictures, some are shapes that began as pictures, and some are pure designs not meant to look like anything. Some change, some stand fast. Some are new and some are very old. Even our letters are symbols, signs that represent a sound, and they came from stylized pictures

fast

slow

locked

unlocked

house sign

Mars
iron
Tuesday
male
staminate
leave control zone

fire: hot

snowflake: cold

sergeant

pineapple: hospitality

of objects that carried that sound in ancient Egypt, or wherever men and women began to write.

Symbols are a vital part of language. To a visitor from China, they are more understandable than written words. To a motorist, they are quicker to "read" and more recognizable at a distance. They are neater and more compact when identifying small switches or parts, and a small symbol can often explain more than a paragraph of directions.

Almost every profession, pursuit, nation, and skill have their own sets of symbols. Some cover many areas with the same meaning, some may stand for many things in many ways, some are singular, one-and-only.

Some signs and devices can become so familiar that we forget they are from the silent language of symbols. The symbols of mathematics are small and powerful, simply but absolutely demanding that we add, subtract, divide, or multiply. We can write a mathematical sentence in words: add fifteen and five and divide the sum by four; the quotient equals five. A very complex sentence, fifty-nine letters and somewhat confusing. We can make the same mathematical statement with ten signs and numerals, thus: $(15 + 5) \div 4 = 5$. This sentence is short, clear, and any second grader in the world can read it and agree with the answer. (It *is* right, isn't it?)

Games have many signs. If you play cards, you are dealing patterns of clubs, hearts, spades, diamonds, jacks, queens, kings, aces—all symbols of value. If you play chess, the sculptured pieces indicate their movement—pawns, rooks, knights, bishops, queens, kings—all symbols. A football coach works out plays in symbolic language. At the Olympic games, signs for the events direct players and spectators. The striped shirts of the referees and the solemn black suits of the umpires are symbols of their functions. Hand signals are important signs.

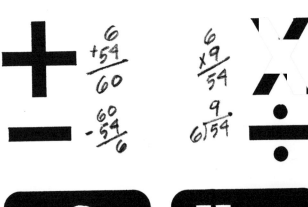

track

fencing

swimming

weight lifting

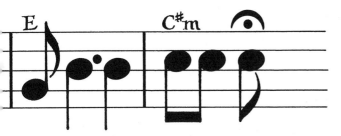

Music is a great achievement of signs. It cannot be "said" in words. It is too complex. Words aren't enough to express the simultaneous sounding by seventy instruments of different notes in different tones. Beethoven set down a symphony in 1808 on a few sheets of paper; today, an orchestra can play the symphony as he heard it—timing, harmony, tones—because musical notation is exact and expressive.

bicycling   equestrian   target shooting   gymnastics

Top: Handle With Care; Side: 16 kilograms gross weight. This Side Up. Capacity 14 liters.

Keep Dry; Fragile; Use No Hooks.

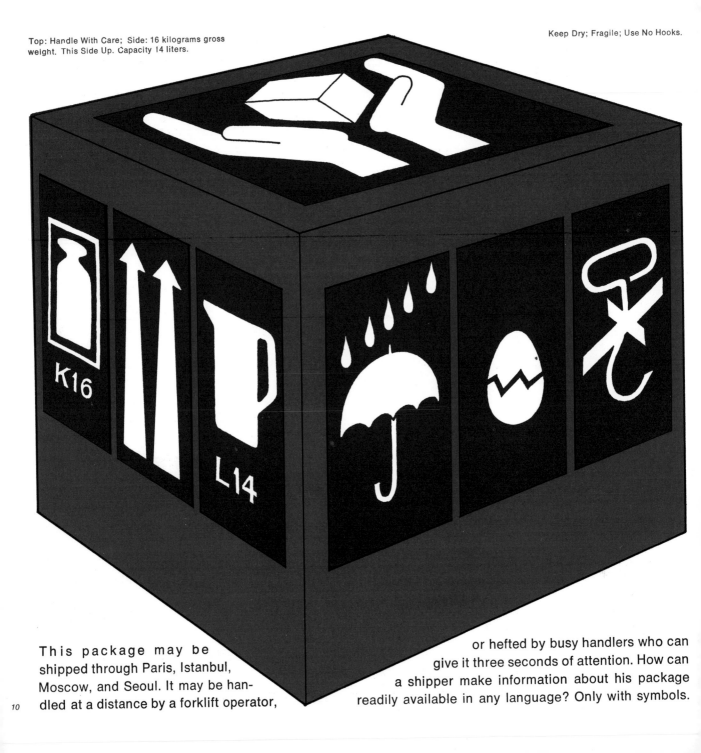

This package may be shipped through Paris, Istanbul, Moscow, and Seoul. It may be handled at a distance by a forklift operator, or hefted by busy handlers who can give it three seconds of attention. How can a shipper make information about his package readily available in any language? Only with symbols.

pirates' Jolly Roger

Signs are insistent, urgent. It is difficult to ignore the skull and crossbones: it reminds us of danger and death. There is a vocabulary of shapes for warning signs: triangles warn of specific hazards; circles restrict or prohibit; squares advise or require. Shapes of danger can be real or abstract: fire can be drawn but the threat of radiation must be symbolized.

poison

warning: sharp

smoking prohibited

gloves must be worn

fire extinguisher

fire

radiation

bio-hazard

laser

corrosive

slippery

electricity

falling objects

12   Lights: bright, fog, parking, dim. Rear window heater, emergency flasher, light dimmer, windshield washer, windshield wiper, vent.

Speed, revolutions, engine temperature, water temperature, oil pressure, battery, transmission oil pressure, fuel, choke, ignition key.

In an international market, one car model might sell in a dozen countries, a dozen languages, but all drivers can read the controls . . . in symbols. And every glove compartment becomes jammed with road maps . . . sheets full of guiding symbols.

Defrost/floor, heat/cool, fan, dome light, volume, tuning.

interstate

national

state

county

traffic light

Locked into a pack of moving cars like one bee in a swarm, the motorist can spare only the flick of an eye for road signs. Their meaning must be clear in that instant, from a distance, through rain and snow and fog. For interstate highways, even the route numbers have a code: odd numbers run mostly north and south, even numbers go east and west; a three-digit number with a "1" prefix connects two interstates; a three-digit number with an even prefix is a belt route around a city; a prefix of 3, 5, 7, or 9 in a three-digit number indicates a spur route, leaving the "parent" route and returning at the same interchange.

stop

yield

speed limit

road configuration

round: U-turn prohibited

round: pedestrians restricted to left side

dim light

motorcycles & cars prohibited

14

falling rock

road work

children

drawbridge

pass with caution

railroad crossing

parking

road divides

road narrows

bumpy road

rotary

motorbikes prohibited

axle load limit: 4 tons

height limit: 3 meters

no parking

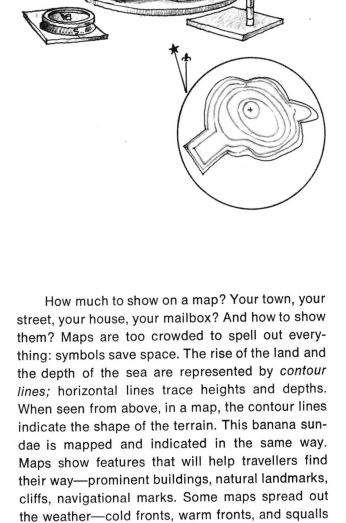

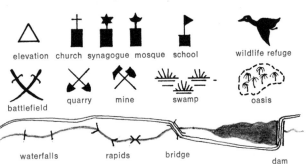

elevation	church	synagogue	mosque	school		wildlife refuge
battlefield	quarry	mine	swamp			oasis

waterfalls	rapids	bridge	dam

How much to show on a map? Your town, your street, your house, your mailbox? And how to show them? Maps are too crowded to spell out everything: symbols save space. The rise of the land and the depth of the sea are represented by *contour lines;* horizontal lines trace heights and depths. When seen from above, in a map, the contour lines indicate the shape of the terrain. This banana sundae is mapped and indicated in the same way. Maps show features that will help travellers find their way—prominent buildings, natural landmarks, cliffs, navigational marks. Some maps spread out the weather—cold fronts, warm fronts, and squalls between—and present it so it can be understood, even anticipated.

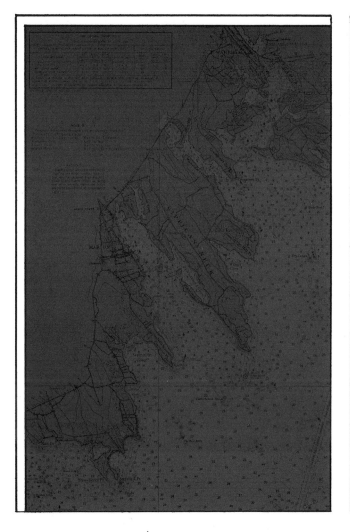

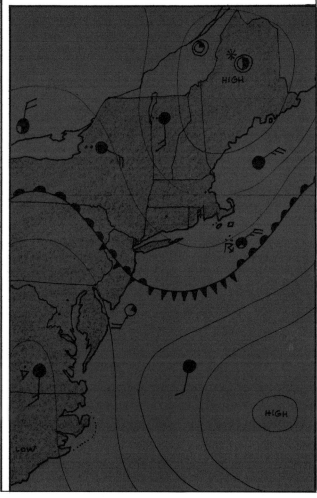

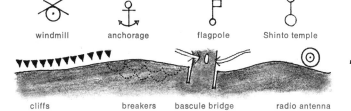

can	nun	beacon	lightship	visible wreck

sunken wreck

windmill	anchorage	flagpole	Shinto temple

cliffs   breakers   bascule bridge   radio antenna

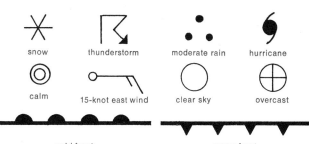

snow	thunderstorm	moderate rain	hurricane
calm	15-knot east wind	clear sky	overcast

cold front   warm front

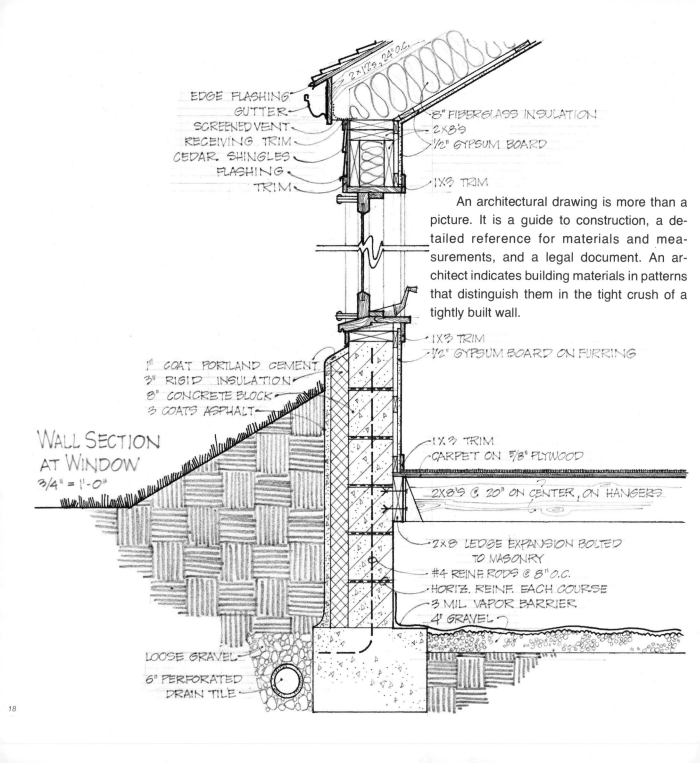

EDGE FLASHING
GUTTER
SCREENED VENT
RECEIVING TRIM
CEDAR SHINGLES
FLASHING
TRIM

2×12's, 24" O.C.

8" FIBERGLASS INSULATION
2×8's
½" GYPSUM BOARD

1×3 TRIM

An architectural drawing is more than a picture. It is a guide to construction, a detailed reference for materials and measurements, and a legal document. An architect indicates building materials in patterns that distinguish them in the tight crush of a tightly built wall.

1×3 TRIM
½" GYPSUM BOARD ON FURRING

1" COAT PORTLAND CEMENT
3" RIGID INSULATION
8" CONCRETE BLOCK
3 COATS ASPHALT

WALL SECTION
AT WINDOW
3/4" = 1'-0"

1×3 TRIM
CARPET ON 5/8" PLYWOOD

2×8'S @ 20" ON CENTER, ON HANGERS

2×8 LEDGE EXPANSION BOLTED
TO MASONRY
#4 REINF. RODS @ 8" O.C.
HORIZ. REINF. EACH COURSE
3 MIL VAPOR BARRIER
4" GRAVEL

LOOSE GRAVEL
6" PERFORATED
DRAIN TILE

cowboy's hat

Mexican sombrero

welder's helmet

fireman's helmet

pilgrim's hat

rice farmer's hat

yarmulka

fez

sailor's cap

ranger's hat

nurse's cap

diver's cap

graduate's mortar board

helmet

Hats become symbols when they are strongly linked to a profession or country or way of life. These hats are very few today compared with an earlier time when butchers wore straw skimmers, chimney sweeps wore stovepipes, bankers wore bowlers, and teamsters wore plugs.

men's lavatory

women's lavatory

restaurant

information

first aid

postbox

telephone

lost and found

baggage check-in

baggage check-out

heliport

currency exchange

car rental

bus stop

handicapped access

observation deck

An international airport: jets from every part of the world touch down and taxi their passengers to the terminal, where strangers speaking a hundred languages mingle, rest, eat, ask questions, rent cars, move on to other jets and other countries —all in a hurry. English, French, German, Spanish, Russian, and Chinese signs might speak to most of them, but not to all—and what a clutter of words! Symbols speak to all travellers, even to those who cannot read, but the designer must use images that are common to all nations. A steak would not be an effective symbol for a restaurant; in most countries, meat is never eaten in such a large piece, and many people eat no meat at all. The trademarks of airlines direct passengers to the proper gates and proudly advertise one of man's greatest accomplishments: flight.

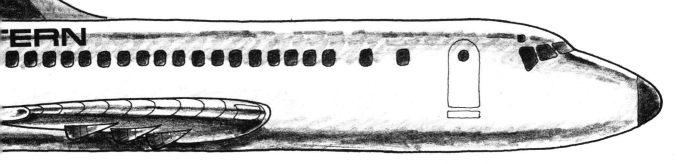

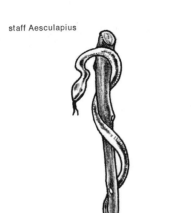

In ancient battles men wandered the fields, giving what first aid they could to the wounded. They carried a sign of their peaceful purpose, the *caduceus*, symbol of the god Mercury, two serpents twined around a winged staff. Earlier, the healing god Aesculapius had been pictured carrying a simple staff with one snake coiled around it. Both images survive as symbols of the healing arts side by side with more modern images like the sign for prescription and the stethoscope. Every hospital is a maze of specialties and services; new images to symbolize them make it less confusing. Perhaps well-designed, pleasant symbols even make a hospital less frightening.

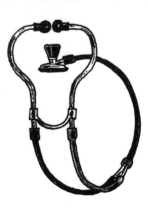

emergency room

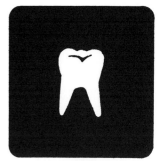
registration

pediatrics

dentistry

laboratory

nurses

physical therapy

cardiology

ophthalmology

psychiatry

speech and hearing

blood bank

nursery

orthopedics

X-ray

surgery

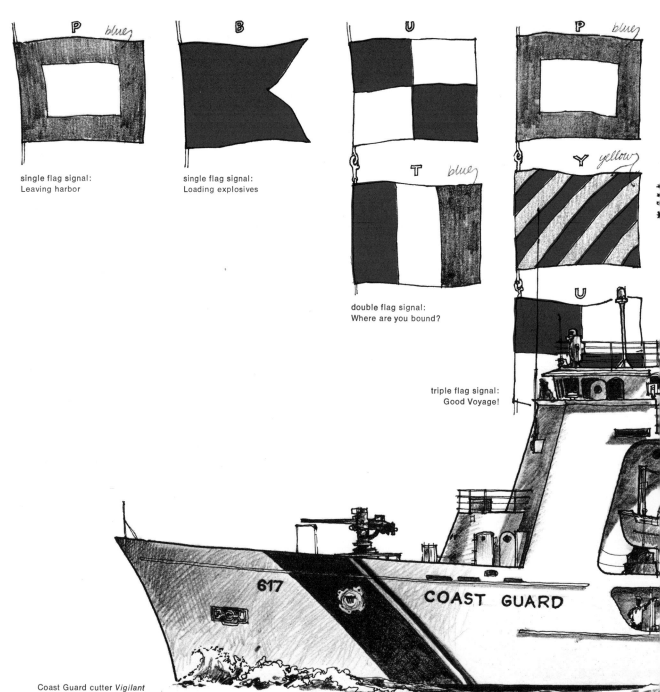

P *blue*

single flag signal:
Leaving harbor

B

single flag signal:
Loading explosives

U

T *blue*

double flag signal:
Where are you bound?

P *blue*

Y *yellow*

U

triple flag signal:
Good Voyage!

617

COAST GUARD

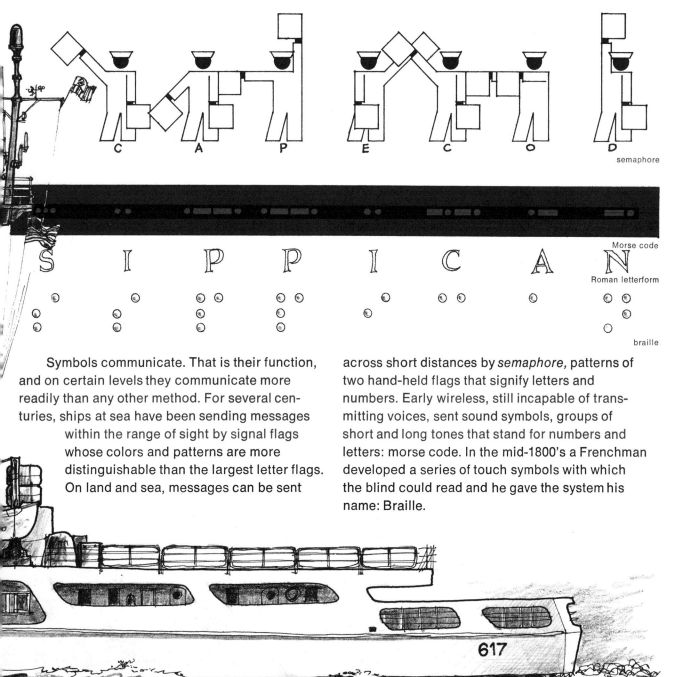

C A P E C O D
semaphore

Morse code

S I P P I C A N
Roman letterform

braille

Symbols communicate. That is their function, and on certain levels they communicate more readily than any other method. For several centuries, ships at sea have been sending messages within the range of sight by signal flags whose colors and patterns are more distinguishable than the largest letter flags. On land and sea, messages can be sent across short distances by *semaphore,* patterns of two hand-held flags that signify letters and numbers. Early wireless, still incapable of transmitting voices, sent sound symbols, groups of short and long tones that stand for numbers and letters: morse code. In the mid-1800's a Frenchman developed a series of touch symbols with which the blind could read and he gave the system his name: Braille.

617

Latin Cross

Orthodox Cross

Coptic Cross

Maltese Cross

the fish

the lamb

Spiritual thinking and writing are full of symbols, signs, codes, and wonders. Jesus Christ and the religions that grew from his example are represented by many symbols: the lamb, the fish, the dove, the anchor, the cross. The cross, central sign of Christianity, has many forms. Judaism has the star of David, the scrolls, the tablets, the menorah. Indeed, every religion seeks to symbolize its beliefs with objects and designs.

the anchor

the dove

Taoist yin-yang

Buddha

Islamic star and crescent

Star of David

Air Force insignia

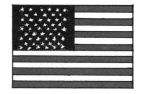

United States flag

United States seal

initials: United States

Knights in battle wore plumes of colored feathers, their own *panache,* that made them more visible to their men at arms. In a struggle, a friend must be distinguished from a foe in an instant: insignia are therefore painted on planes, tanks, trucks, and football helmets. Each nation has many symbols, but the most compact and the easiest to recognize are their military insignia.

red star on a Russian T-32 tank

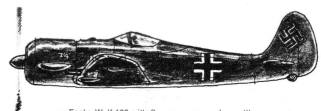

Focke-Wulf 190 with German cross and swastika

Israeli star

Russian hammer and sickle

Canadian maple leaf

Japanese rising sun

27

Cleopatra's cartouche

Japanese emperor's seal

Japanese seal

Richard Lion-Heart

Medici

Leopard passant

Benvenuto Cellini

Pippin the Short

Charlemagne

Ottho the Great

What does it mean to leave your mark? To put the stamp of your personality on events and changes? Great and terrible men, women, families, and dynasties have left the mark of their actions on their times, and have left the mark of their names on buildings, documents, armor, cattle. When the ability to read was rare, marks, signets, coats of arms, seals, monograms, and brands stood for names. The Egyptian mark of a king or queen was a *cartouche*. Noble Japanese families favored simple seals, restrained and beautiful designs. The complex ties of family obligation in feudalism necessitated a complex system of identity called *heraldry,* symbols and images on coats of arms,

Albrecht Dürer

Michelangelo

Martin Luther

Bridle Bit brand

American Indian brand

W. F. Cody

Rocking R

Bob-on-the-square

which began with the insignia on battle shields. Rulers signed orders and documents with *signets,* rings, or seals to make an impression in wax, or by forming their mark with a pen. Some kings were illiterate: King Pippin made the cross of his monogram and scribes added the dots; Charlemagne made a small diamond and scribes added the letters. The great ranchers of the American West were not unlike the great families of Europe, and ranch brands served the same function as the coats of arms and housemarks: They marked property and spoke to people—often illiterate—at a distance, through rain and smoke.

register mark

Walker and Company

Antilles Yachting Services

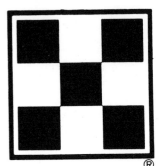
Ralston Purina Co.

Johns-Manville

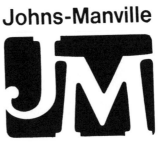
Johns-Manville

PPG
INDUSTRIES
PPG Industries

Trademarks are a vital and contemporary flowering of symbols. They croon to us from super-market shelves, jingle at us from TV screens, shout from banners, soberly stand on magazine pages. One designer vies to be more balanced and appealing than another, to state simply, cleanly, plainly, and forcefully what is meant. What talent of art bent to woo and remind our eyes as we pass busily, as we drive past in the rain, as we flip the page! All the virtues of symbols are here: compact-ness, speed of recognition, legibility at a distance or through difficult circumstances, and, moreover, the ability to sum up, to let an image stand for much behind it—a nation behind a star, an industry behind a bell. You see so many symbols around you—what are your symbols? Your images, mono-grams, insignia, codes, what is your panache? How will you make your mark?

Public Broadcasting Service

Reynolds Aluminum

Playboy, Inc.

International Business Machines

®

PepsiCo, Inc.

Greyhound Bus Lines

Chase Manhattan Bank

Hallmark Cards Incorporated

The Holliston Mills

Quaker Oats

Woodland Boat

Kreeger & Sons

American Telephone & Telegraph Co.

Alling and Cory

There are many families of symbols we have not touched on, fascinating forms that help men and women visualize and work. Here are some books that have helped me gather symbols and signs and will, I think, please and interest you.

Symbol Sourcebook, Henry Dreyfuss, McGraw-Hill
Symbols, Signs & Signets, Ernst Lehner, Dover
Handbook of Pictorial Symbols, Rudolf Modley, Dover
The Book of Signs, Rudolf Koch, Dover
American Trademark Designs, Barbara Baer Capitman, Dover

The Publisher wishes to thank the following for permission to use their trademarks in this book:

Alling and Cory
American Telephone and
 Telegraph
Antilles Yachting Services
Chase Manhattan Bank
Columbia Broadcasting
 System
Eastern Airlines
The Greyhound Corporation
 (The Running Dog is a
 registered trademark of the
 Greyhound Corporation)
Hallmark Cards Incorporated
The Holliston Mills
International Business
 Machines Corp.
Johns Manville Corp.
Kreeger & Sons
National Airlines, Inc.
PPG Industries, Inc.
PepsiCo (Pepsi Cola® (or
 Pepsi®), Which Appears On
 Page 31, Is A Registered
 Trademark And Is
 Reproduced With The
 Permission Of Its Owner
 PepsiCo, Inc.)
Playboy Enterprises (RABBIT
 HEAD Design is a mark of and
 used with permission of
 Playboy, Reg. U. S. Pat. Off.)
Public Broadcasting Service
The Quaker Oats Company
Ralston Purina Company
Reynolds Metals Company
Trans World Airlines, Inc.
Walker and Company
Woodland Boat